MERIDA (MEXICO) TRAVEL GUIDE 2023-2024:

Immerse Yourself in Merida's Vibrant Traditions, Authentic Charm, Cultural Richness and Flavors.

Greene Annabella

Copyright © 2023 by Greene Annabella

All rights reserved. No part of this publication may be reproduced, stored in a retrieval system, or transmitted, in any form or by any means, electronic, mechanical, photocopying, recording, or otherwise, without the prior written permission of the publisher, except for brief quotations in critical reviews or articles.

This book is sold subject to the condition that it shall not, by way of trade or otherwise, be lent, re-sold, hired out, or otherwise circulated without the publisher's prior consent in any form of binding or cover other than that in which it is published and without a similar condition including this condition being imposed on the subsequent purchaser.

Table of Content

INTRODUCTION 6
CHAPTER ONE 14
   Making Travel Plans 14
      When is the best time to visit Merida? 14
   Travel Tips and Essential Information 16
   Entry Regulations and Visa Requirements 21
   What to Bring and What to Pack 24
   Precautions for Health and Safety 29
   Interesting Reasons to Visit 34
   Things You Should Never Do 38
CHAPTER TWO 43
   Getting to Merida 43
      Airports and Transportation Options 43
      Travel Routes Suggestions 50
   Accommodation Options 55
      Hotels and Resorts 55
   Stay Experiences That Are One-of-a-Kind 59
CHAPTER THREE 64
   Merida's Culinary Delights 64
      Traditional Yucatecan Cuisine 64
   Popular restaurants and grocery stores 68
   Merida's Food Markets 70
   Street Food and Must-Try Dishes 72
CHAPTER FOUR 76
   Exploring Merida 76
      Overview of Merida's History and Culture. 76

Top Tourist Attractions..................................84
Hidden Gems and Off-the-Beaten-Path Spots.... 107
Natural Reserves and Parks..........................111

CHAPTER FIVE..**116**
Shopping in Merida.. 116

CHAPTER SIX..**124**
Nightlife and Entertainment..........................124
    Bars, Clubs, and Live Music Venues........124
Festivals and cultural events..........................128

CHAPTER SEVEN.. **133**
Outdoor Activities and Adventure................. 133
    Eco-Tours and Nature Excursions............133
Water Sports and Beach Activities................137
Day Trips and Excursions.............................. 142
Photography Tips... 153
    Capturing the Best of Merida's Landscapes.. 153

CHAPTER EIGHT...**162**
Art and Culture Scene....................................162
    Galleries and Art Exhibitions................... 162
    Folklore and traditional performances..... 166
Merida with Kids..171
    Family-Friendly Attractions and Activities..... 171
    Tips for Childcare and Safety................... 176

CHAPTER NINE... **181**
Health and Wellness...................................... 181
    Spas and Wellness Centers..................... 181
Retreats for Yoga and Meditation.................185

CHAPTER TEN..**189**
　Practical Information................................... 189
　Local Customs and Etiquette................... 189
　Basic Phrases and Expressions....................193
　Currency and Banking Services...............197
CONCLUSION..**201**

INTRODUCTION

Merida, located in the heart of Mexico's Yucatan Peninsula, is a city rich in history and culture. As soon as I stepped foot in this magnificent city, I knew I was about to embark on a once-in-a-lifetime adventure.

It all started when I arrived at Merida's international airport and was met by a pleasant wind whispering stories of the city's history. The architectural marvels that loomed tall on each side attracted me the instant I walked into the cobblestone lanes. The colorful façade of colonial-period buildings appeared to whisper tales of a bygone age.

I spent my time in Merida exploring its gorgeous plazas and lively marketplaces. The city's main plaza, Plaza Grande, was a swarm of activity. Passers-by were amused by street entertainers, while local artists showcased their unique creations. The sweet sounds of marimbas filled the air, creating a lovely ambiance.

The Mayan World Museum in Merida was one of the highlights of my vacation. The museum's displays eloquently displayed the Mayan civilization's rich history and culture. I felt a strong connection to the past as I stared at old relics and learnt about the city's links to this ancient civilisation.

The historical tour was completed with a visit to the neighboring Dzibilchaltun Archaeological Site. The ancient remains, which date back thousands of years, rose majestically in the middle of luxuriant foliage. I couldn't help but think of the Mayans who previously flourished in this precise spot.

Merida's food scene was a sensory overload. I savored the tastes of Yucatecan food, such as cochinita pibil and papadzules. The crowded Mercado Lucas de Galvez provided a genuine experience, with odors of freshly prepared street food filling the air and enticing my taste senses.

To escape the heat of the day, I went to the city's cenotes, which are natural sinkholes filled with crystalline water. Cenote Suytun was a captivating sight, with sunlight flowing through a natural hole in the cavern's roof and throwing an ethereal glow on the blue waters below.

As the sun began to set, I ventured out into Merida's lively nightlife. At a noisy bar, I joined locals and other foreigners in a salsa dance, embracing the irresistible rhythms that filled the air. The night was a symphony of laughing and companionship, making it one of the most memorable of my vacation.

I took a day excursion to Chichen Itza, a UNESCO World Heritage Site, one morning. Against the beautiful blue sky, the mighty pyramids and the Temple of Kukulkan stood majestically. The complexities of this ancient masterpiece were uncovered by a competent guide, leaving me in awe of the Mayans' architectural brilliance.

Throughout my travels, I was met with the kindness and friendliness of the locals. Their sincere smiles and friendly gestures made me feel more like a guest than a visitor. Their anecdotes, exchanged over cups of genuine Yucatecan chocolate, made my visit to Merida absolutely unforgettable.

As my time in Merida came to an end, I realized I had seen something incredible. Not only had the city given me wonderful experiences, but it had also given me a better appreciation for the rich tapestry of history and culture woven into its streets.

It was difficult to leave Merida, but I knew that a piece of this colorful city would live on in my heart forever. So, with a vow to return someday, I waved goodbye to the city that had provided me with a really amazing and enlightening experience - a voyage I would remember for the rest of my life.

Welcome to the engrossing world of "Melinda Travel Guide 2023 and Beyond"! We are thrilled to have you join us on this expedition as we discover the hidden jewels and treasures that await you in Melinda's wonderful city.

We've included a wealth of information in this thorough guide to make your vacation memorable. Whether you're a seasoned traveler or a first-time visitor, our goal is to give you with a rich mine of information, suggestions, and recommendations that will improve every aspect of your Melinda experience.

Melinda provides a combination of heritage and modernity that will fascinate your senses, from historical treasures that whisper tales of the past to contemporary joys that embrace the future. Melinda offers something unique for every tourist, whether it's meandering through bustling markets, savoring in wonderful food, or immersing yourself in local culture.

Prepare to be amazed by stunning scenery and to meet warm-hearted natives who will welcome you with open arms. Our guide will walk you through the complexities of navigating this wonderful city, ensuring that you make the most of your visit and create treasured experiences that will last a lifetime.

So pack your luggage, open your heart to adventure, and prepare to discover Melinda's many delights. Allow our travel guide to be your faithful companion, taking you through every step of your trip and revealing the beauty that awaits you around every corner.

We hope you discover inspiration, excitement, and awe as you read through the "Melinda Travel Guide 2023 and Beyond." May your journeys bring you pleasure, discovery, and unique experiences.

Good luck and welcome to Melinda!

CHAPTER ONE

Making Travel Plans

When is the best time to visit Merida?

The dry season, which lasts from November to April, is the finest time to visit Merida, Mexico. This time of year has nice weather with low humidity and little rain, making it perfect for visiting the city and its surrounds. Temperatures range from the mid-60s to the mid-80s Fahrenheit (18°C to 30°C) at this time of year.

If you want to skip the main tourist season, try visiting Merida between November and April. These months provide nice weather and less people, enabling you to experience the city's attractions and activities at a slower pace.

If you like vivid cultural events and festivals, try visiting Merida during its annual Carnival in February or the Day of the Dead celebration in early November. These events highlight the city's rich traditions while also providing unique insights into its local culture.

Keep in mind that Merida may be fairly hot and humid from May to October, with temperatures often reaching the upper 90s Fahrenheit (over 30°C). While this time of year may be less busy and more economical, be prepared for afternoon rains and greater humidity levels.

Travel Tips and Essential Information

Before you go off on your excursion, here are some useful travel tips and information to help you have a safe and pleasurable voyage.

Visa and Entry Requirements:

Before going to Mexico, check the visa requirements for your nationality. Check that your passport is valid for at least six months beyond the duration of your anticipated stay.

ideal Time to Visit:

The ideal time to visit Melinda is from November to April, when the weather is nice and there are less rain showers.

Health & immunizations:

Before your travel, make sure you have all of your usual immunizations up to date. Consult a travel health specialist for further immunizations and advice tailored to your individual trip plans.

Travel insurance:

Purchase comprehensive travel insurance that includes coverage for medical emergencies, trip cancellations, and lost or stolen possessions.

Currency & Money:
The Mexican Peso (MXN) is the country's official currency. ATMs are commonly accessible in Melinda, and most businesses take major credit cards.

Language:
Spanish is the official language of Mexico. While many inhabitants in tourist destinations understand English, knowing a few basic Spanish words may be beneficial and welcomed.

Safety precautions:
Melinda is typically safe for tourists, but employ care in busy locations and common sense to secure your possessions. Keep an eye

on your valuables and avoid flaunting pricey stuff.

Local Transportation:

Melinda has a substantial public transit infrastructure, which includes buses and taxis. For enhanced security, use certified taxis with appropriate signs or utilize ride-sharing applications.

Accommodation:

Plan ahead of time, particularly during busy seasons, to acquire the greatest alternatives and costs. Melinda has a wide range of housing choices, ranging from boutique hotels to lovely guesthouses.

Cultural Acceptance and appreciate:

Accept and appreciate the local culture and traditions. Dress modestly and follow photography rules while visiting religious places.

Local cuisine:
Traditional Yucatecan delicacies such as cochinita pibil, panuchos, and sopa de lima should not be missed. For a really genuine cuisine experience, visit local markets and street food booths.

Sun Protection:
Because the weather in Melinda may be hot and sunny, bring sunscreen, sunglasses, and a wide-brimmed hat to protect yourself from the sun's rays.

Tap water:
To prevent the danger of waterborne infections, it is suggested that you use bottled water in Melinda. Brush your teeth with bottled water as well.

Emergencies:

In case of an emergency, memorize or preserve the local emergency phone numbers for police, medical services, and your country's embassy or consulate.

Local Events and Festivals:

Consult local event calendars to determine if any festivals or cultural events are scheduled during your stay. Participating in these festivals might give you a fresh perspective on Melinda's customs.

By keeping these travel tips and important facts in mind, you can make the most of your trip to Melinda and create wonderful experiences. Have a wonderful trip!

Entry Regulations and Visa Requirements

The visa requirements and entrance procedures for Merida, Mexico differ depending on your country. Here's some background information:

Visa Requirements:

Visas are not required for citizens of several countries, including the United States, Canada, the European Union, Australia, and others, for stays of up to 180 days for tourist, business, or family visits.

Tourist Card (FMM):

Visitors arriving in Mexico by plane or cruise ship may be required to complete a Forma Migratoria Mltiple (FMM), commonly known as a tourist card. The FMM is normally granted upon arrival and enables for stays of up to 180 days.

Passport Requirements:
Make sure your passport is valid for at least six months beyond the duration of your anticipated stay in Mexico.

Border Crossing:
If you arrive by land, one may be required to stop at a border crossing to receive an FMM.

Visa Extensions:
If you want to remain longer than the original 180 days, you may apply for an extension at the Instituto Nacional de Migración (INM) office in Mexico.

Other Visa Requirements:
If your visit includes working, studying, or indulging in other activities not covered by the

tourist visa, you may need to apply for a separate visa or permission before going to Mexico.

What to Bring and What to Pack

clothes:

Lightweight, breathable clothes appropriate for warm weather.

T-shirts, tank tops, and shorts are appropriate for daytime activities.

For chilly nights, a light jacket or shawl.

Walking shoes that are comfortable for visiting the city and its attractions.

For informal trips and beach vacations, wear sandals or flip-flops.

If you want to visit cenotes or beaches, bring a swimsuit.

Sun Protection:

Use a sunscreen with a high SPF to protect yourself from the sun.

Wear a hat with a wide brim and sunglasses to protect your face and eyes.

A lightweight, long-sleeved shirt for protection from the sun during peak hours.

Travel Essentials:

Passport and other appropriate travel papers are required.

Chargers and travel adapters for your electrical gadgets.

Portable power bank for charging your electronics on the road.

A day bag or backpack for taking items on vacations.

drugs and medical supplies:

Prescription drugs, as well as a copy of the prescription.

A basic first-aid package that includes bandages, antiseptic cream, and pain medications.

Insect repellant to keep mosquitos and other insects at bay.

Personal Hygiene:

Toiletries such as a toothbrush, toothpaste, shampoo, and soap are examples of personal hygiene.

For on-the-go cleaning, use hand sanitizer or wet wipes.

Documents and copies:

Make copies of key papers, such as your passport, visa, and travel insurance. Separate them from the originals.

Cash and Cards:

Mexican Pesos are generally accepted for modest transactions and tipping (however major credit cards are not).

Internationally compatible debit/credit cards.

Memory Cards and Camera:

Bring a camera or smartphone to record the amazing moments in Merida.

Extra memory cards or external storage are recommended for storing your images.

Guidebook or Travel App:

A trip guidebook or travel app provides information about Merida's sights and culture.

Download travel applications that include maps, language translation, and local suggestions.

Water Bottle:

Bring a reusable water bottle to remain hydrated while reducing plastic waste.

Spanish Phrasebook or translation:

For conversation, a pocket-sized Spanish phrasebook or language translation app might be useful.

Remember that Merida can become fairly hot, particularly in the summer, so bring light, breathable clothes to remain cool. Keep a refillable water bottle on hand and drink lots of water to remain hydrated in the hot weather.

Finally, make room in your suitcase for souvenirs and handicrafts to take home as mementos of your unforgettable trip to Merida!

Precautions for Health and Safety

When visiting Merida, Mexico, it is important to emphasize health and safety in order to have a nice and worry-free trip. Here are some measures to take for your health and safety:

Vaccinations and Health Examination:

Consult your doctor about any required vaccines or health precautions for Mexico and the Yucatan Peninsula.

Safe Drinking Water:

To prevent waterborne infections, drink and wash your teeth with bottled water.

Food Safety:

While you should enjoy the local cuisine, be aware of street food and make sure it's freshly made and served hot.

Consume no raw or undercooked meals.

Sun Protection:

The sun may be harsh in Merida, so protect yourself from damaging UV rays by using sunscreen with a high SPF, a wide-brimmed hat, and sunglasses.

Insect Protection:

Insect repellent should be used to protect against mosquito bites, particularly in the evening.

keep Hydrated:

Drink lots of water, particularly in hot weather, to keep hydrated and avoid heat-related problems.

Travel insurance:

Purchase comprehensive travel insurance that includes medical emergencies and evacuation.

Safety in Public spaces:

To discourage possible theft, be careful with your valuables and avoid exhibiting costly goods in popular locations.

Emergency Number:

Local emergency contact numbers for police, medical services, and your country's embassy or consulate should be saved.

Transportation Safety:

For safer transportation, choose authorized taxis with clear signs or ride-sharing services.

Covid 19 precautions:

Check for the most recent COVID-19 travel standards and restrictions for Mexico and Merida.

Follow local health rules, use masks in public places if necessary, and keep a physical distance.

Respect Local Customs and Laws:

To guarantee a happy stay, be respectful of local customs and traditions and follow Mexican laws.

Traveling Alone:

If you are traveling alone, advise someone back home of your schedule and keep in touch with them on a frequent basis.

Emergency preparedness:

Prepare for an emergency by familiarizing yourself with the layout of your accommodation and the nearby exits in case of an emergency.

You may have a worry-free and delightful vacation to Merida if you are aware of these health and safety considerations. Embrace the local culture, see the city's treasures, and make unforgettable memories while putting your health first.

Interesting Reasons to Visit

There are several fascinating reasons to visit Merida, making it a popular tourist destination. Here are some convincing reasons why Merida is a must-see city:

Historical splendor: With its colonial architecture, well-preserved buildings, and attractive streets, Merida is steeped in history. The magnificence of the city reflects its history, providing a look into its colonial and Mayan origins.

Mayan Mystique: Merida, located in the middle of the Yucatan Peninsula, serves as a gateway to various Mayan historic sites and ruins. Exploring ancient towns like Chichen Itza and Uxmal allows you to learn more about this intriguing civilisation.

Cultural Fusion: Merida is a cultural melting pot of Spanish and Mayan civilizations, resulting in a complex tapestry of customs, art, music, and gastronomy. This synthesis is seen in many aspects of everyday life, producing a dynamic and diversified environment.

Warm Hospitality: The people of Merida are well-known for their friendliness. Locals take delight in sharing their culture with guests, providing a really welcoming experience that leaves an indelible impression.

Paseo de Montejo: This majestic avenue, which is sometimes likened to Paris' Champs-Élysées, has exquisite houses, ancient structures, and tree-lined streets. A stroll along Paseo de Montejo provides a peek of Merida's former splendor.

Culinary Delights: Yucatecan cuisine is a sensory delight. From savory cochinita pibil to refreshing ceviche, you'll go on a gastronomic journey highlighting distinct tastes and customs.

Festivals & Events: Throughout the year, Merida is alive with festivals and events. You'll get the opportunity to immerse yourself in local customs and festivals, from the vivid Day of the Dead celebrations to the mesmerizing Hanal Pixan.

Art and Culture Scene: Merida's art and culture scene is growing, with vibrant art galleries, museums, and cultural institutions. You may discover modern art, traditional crafts, and get immersed in the creative essence of the city.

Wellness and Relaxation: Merida provides quiet locations for relaxation and regeneration, from yoga retreats to spa treatments. Disconnect from the outside world and discover peace in the city's peaceful havens.

Gateway to Natural Beauty: Beyond the city, the Yucatan Peninsula expands with lush forests, crystal-clear cenotes, and breathtaking coastal locations. The location of Merida enables you to enjoy the region's numerous natural attractions.

Each of these factors adds to Merida's attractiveness, making it a place that entices visitors to explore its history, culture, cuisines, and experiences. Merida offers a spectacular experience that will long retain a particular place in your heart, whether you are lured by its architectural wonders, cultural tapestry, or the opportunity to discover ancient secrets.

Things You Should Never Do

It is essential to respect the local culture and traditions when visiting Merida. To guarantee a good and harmonious encounter, avoid the following behaviors:

Disregard Local Customs and Traditions: Always respect local customs and traditions, particularly during festivals and ceremonies. Avoid disrupting or insulting traditions that are important to the community.

Personal Space: Mexicans place a high emphasis on personal space. Avoid standing too near to people in public places, and always get permission before photographing someone.

Littering: Help keep the city clean by properly disposing of your rubbish. Avoid littering in public places or natural environments, and instead use designated garbage cans.

Public intoxication: Drink sensibly while enjoying the nightlife. Public drunkenness is frowned upon and might cause problems.

Engage in unlawful Activities: It is unlawful in Mexico to use or possess narcotics. Such conduct may have substantial legal ramifications.

Disrespect Religious Sites: Be courteous while visiting churches or temples. Avoid having loud discussions, snapping pictures during ceremonies, and engaging in unacceptable conduct.

Insensitive Dressing: Dress modestly while visiting religious places or local communities to show respect. In such situations, avoid wearing exposing attire.

Excessive negotiating: While negotiating is usual in marketplaces, avoid being combative. Remember that merchants depend on reasonable pricing to make a living.

Speak Loudly: It is considered rude to speak loudly in public settings such as restaurants and public transit.

Assume Everyone Speaks English: While English is used in tourist regions, it is polite to learn simple phrases in Spanish or Yucatec Maya in order to interact properly.

Ignore Safety Precautions: When swimming in cenotes, the sea, or participating in outdoor activities, follow safety recommendations and precautions. Ignoring safety precautions may result in an accident.

Overindulge in Alcohol: Moderate your alcohol intake while enjoying local beverages to protect your safety and well-being.

Excessive Public Displays of Affection: While holding hands is permitted, excessive public displays of affection may make locals uncomfortable.

Avoiding these practices and showing respect for the local culture will result in more pleasant encounters and a more pleasurable trip for both you and the Merida community.

CHAPTER TWO

Getting to Merida

Airports and Transportation Options

Getting to Merida, Mexico, is reasonably simple due to the city's excellent domestic and international transportation connections. Here's a map of how to get to Merida:

By Air: The international airport in Merida is known as "Manuel Crescencio Rejón International Airport" (IATA: MID). It handles local as well as foreign flights.

Direct flights to Merida are available from major Mexican cities as well as some US locations. Check with airlines for schedules and availability.

Domestic Flights: If you are already in Mexico, you may fly to Merida from major cities such as Mexico City, Cancun, Guadalajara, and Monterrey, among others.

International Flights: If you are coming from another country, check for direct flights to Merida from places such as Miami, Houston, and Fort Lauderdale, as well as other international locations.

Transportation from the Airport: You may easily locate taxis and approved shuttle services to transport you to your hotel or lodging from Manuel Crescencio Rejón International Airport. Many hotels also provide airport transportation, so check with your hotel ahead of time.

By Bus: Merida has an extensive bus network that connects it to cities across Mexico. Luxury and first-class buses provide pleasant and secure transportation.

ADO, ETN, and Oriente are among the bus companies that provide trips to Merida.

By vehicle: If you prefer to drive, you may hire a vehicle in Mexico from major cities and airports. Highways link Merida, and the road infrastructure is typically in excellent shape.

When deciding on the best mode of transportation for your trip to Merida, consider aspects such as money, journey time, and convenience. Whether you come by flight, bus, or vehicle, Merida's warm warmth and rich cultural legacy will greet you.

Merida Public Transportation
Local transportation is easily accessible in Merida, making it easy for travelers to explore

the city and its surrounds. The following are the main means of local transportation in Merida:

Buses for the Public:

Merida has a comprehensive public bus system that serves the majority of the city. Buses are an inexpensive mode of transportation that connects to main sites and areas.

For routes inside the city center, look for buses bearing "Circuito Centro" (downtown circuit) signage.

Bikes for the environment (Bici-Ruta):

Bici-Ruta, Merida's bike-sharing program, enables you to borrow bicycles for short rides throughout the city.

Look for bike stations across the city where you may pick up and drop off your bike.

Taxis:

Taxis are a common means of transportation in Merida, and they can be found all around the city. Official taxis are typically yellow and have a specific symbol on the side.

It is encouraged to utilize approved taxis or ride-sharing services such as Uber for safety and cost transparency.

Rent a car:

If you prefer the freedom of driving, you can hire a vehicle in Merida from one of the many car rental firms. Having a vehicle allows you to explore the surrounding places at your own speed.

Horse-Drawn Vehicles:

Horse-drawn carriages, known as "calesas," may be found in Merida's historic center, providing a pleasant and relaxing way to observe the city's colonial architecture.

Colectivos:

Colectivos are shared vans or minivans that run on predetermined routes inside the city as well as to surrounding towns and attractions. They are a cost-effective solution for short trips.

Bikes and scooters for rent:

Some businesses hire out bikes and electric scooters, making it a pleasant and environmentally responsible way to explore Merida's streets.

The city is quite simple to navigate, and residents are often happy to assist with instructions if required. Because English may not be widely spoken by everyone, it's a good idea to have some basic Spanish phrases on hand for conversation.

Each mode of transportation provides a distinct experience, enabling you to immerse yourself in Merida's vivid culture and ambiance. Whether you take the bus, ride your bike through the streets, or take a cab, travelling about the city is part of the fun!

Travel Routes Suggestions

There are various suggested travel itineraries for touring Merida and its neighboring locations that may provide a unique and rewarding experience. Consider the following travel options:

Walking Tour of Historic Merida: Begin your adventure in the heart of the city with a walking tour of Merida's historic center. Visit Plaza Grande, San Ildefonso Cathedral, and the Palacio de Gobierno. Discover Paseo de Montejo, a huge road surrounded with beautiful houses and sculptures.

Route to the Mayan Ruins and Cenotes: Take a day excursion to neighboring Mayan ruins and cenotes. Explore the awe-inspiring ancient city of Chichen Itza, one of the New Seven Wonders of the World. After that, relax in a neighboring cenote such as Ik Kil or Cenote Hubiku.

Uxmal and the Puuc Route: Explore the Puuc Route, which contains the ancient city of Uxmal as well as other Puuc-style archaeological monuments. Admire the exquisite masonry and architecture that is distinctive to this area.

Celestun & Flamingo Watching: Visit the Celestun Biosphere Reserve, a nature sanctuary and home to a large number of flamingos. Take a boat cruise to see these magnificent birds in their natural environment.

Izamal, the Yellow City: Visit Izamal, a lovely town famed for its yellow-painted houses and the gorgeous Franciscan monastery, Convento de San Antonio de Padua.

Valladolid and Ek Balam: Visit Valladolid, a colonial town with colorful streets and ancient structures. Visit Ek Balam, a magnificent Mayan archaeological site with a well-preserved acropolis.

caverns and Cenotes expedition: Set off on a subterranean expedition to discover the region's cenotes and caverns. For a one-of-a-kind experience, consider visiting Cenote X'batun or Cenote Dzitnup.

Hacienda Tour: Take a tour of classic haciendas to learn about the history of the Yucatan's henequen period. Learn about henequen production and the estates' fascinating history.

Food & Culinary Journey: Take a culinary journey through Merida's bustling food scene. Local Yucatecan cuisine can be found at markets, street food vendors, and traditional restaurants.

Circuit of Arts and Culture: Immerse yourself in the city's arts and culture by visiting galleries, art centers, and cultural events and performances.

Remember to plan your trip itineraries based on your interests, time constraints, and transit alternatives. Each route provides a distinct perspective on Merida's rich history, natural beauty, and cultural legacy, ensuring that your visit is memorable and fulfilling.

Accommodation Options

Hotels and Resorts

Luxury Hotels and Resorts:

Hyatt Regency Merida: This luxury hotel in the city center provides contemporary facilities and a rooftop pool. Avenida Colon 450, Merida, Yucatan.

Fiesta Americana Merida: An attractive hotel featuring on-site restaurants and a fitness facility. Paseo de Montejo 451, Merida, Yucatán.

Hacienda Xcanatun: A beautiful boutique hotel housed in a rebuilt 18th-century hacienda with a quiet and romantic ambience. Calle 20 S/N Comisara Xcanatun, Merida, Yucatan.

Hotels in the Mid-Range:

Hotel El Conquistador: A decent hotel in a convenient position near several attractions. Calle 56 #468, between 55 and 57, Merida, Yucatan.

Hotel Casa Lucia: A beautiful colonial-style boutique hotel with a courtyard pool. Calle 60, Nos. 474 x 53 y 55, Merida, Yucatan.

Hotel Casa del Balam: A historic hotel with a traditional ambience in the city's centre. Calle 57, No. 481, Merida, Yucatan.

Budget and Hostel Accommodations:

Nomadas Hostel: A well-known hostel with a relaxed environment and social activities. Calle 62 #433, Merida, Yucatan, Mexico.

Casa Nico Hostal: A pleasant hostel with helpful staff and a convenient location. Calle 47, No. 480, Merida, Yucatan.

Casona 61: is a low-cost guesthouse with a lovely courtyard and reasonably priced rooms. Calle 61, No. 499, Merida, Yucatan.

Hostal Zocalo: is located in Calle 63, No. 506, Merida, Yucatan.
The hotel is located in the city's centre, only steps away from the main plaza and the city's active nightlife.
Transportation: Taxis are widely accessible at the airport and bus station. Because to its prominent position, many drivers are familiar with Hostal Zocalo.

Hostal Catedral :is located in Calle 55, No. 511 in Merida, Yucatan.

The Cathedral of Merida and other city attractions are nearby.

Taxis are accessible at both the airport and the bus terminal. The hostel is a short distance away from these places of arrival.

It is pretty simple to get to these lodgings from the airport or bus terminals. Taxis are widely accessible at the airport, and many hotels provide airport transfers on request. You may also take a local bus or colectivo from the bus terminal to the city center to save money.

Stay Experiences That Are One-of-a-Kind

When visiting Merida, Mexico, you may enjoy unique stay experiences that go beyond standard hotels. Here are some unusual hotel alternatives that can make your visit to Merida genuinely memorable:

Hacienda: Stay at a restored Hacienda, which were old colonial-era estates with beautiful grounds and historical charm. Haciendas provide a real peek into the history and culture of the area.

Boutique hotel: Merida is well-known for its stunning boutique hotels situated in refurbished colonial structures. These homes often include distinctive architectural characteristics, elegant décor, and individualized service.

Eco-Lodges & Sustainable Retreats: Stay at eco-lodges or sustainable retreats to experience the natural splendor of the Yucatan Peninsula. These lodgings include eco-friendly practices, natural immersion, and adventure options.

Cenote Lodge:Some hotels and resorts are built around cenotes, which are natural sinkholes filled with crystal-clear water. Staying near a cenote provides you with tranquil settings and easy access to this natural treasure.

Glamping: Choose a glamping trip to embrace nature without compromising comfort. In the middle of the Yucatecan scenery, stay in magnificent tents or cabins outfitted with contemporary comforts.

Artistic Retreats: Some Merida lodgings are created to be artistic retreats, where you may participate in creative seminars, art lessons, or cultural events.

Casa Particulares: These are private guesthouses or rooms in local households. Staying in one enables you to experience genuine Yucatecan hospitality while learning about the local way of life.

Yoga & Wellness Retreats: Merida has a number of yoga and wellness retreats that concentrate on regeneration, relaxation, and overall well-being.

Temazcal Lodges: Staying at a Temazcal lodge allows you to participate in traditional Mayan ceremonies. A sweat lodge is used in Temazcal rites for cleansing and spiritual regeneration.

Farm Stays: For a really authentic rural experience, try staying on a traditional Yucatecan farm where you can participate in agricultural activities, learn about sustainable techniques, and eat fresh local vegetables.

Each distinct stay experience provides a unique perspective on Merida's culture, environment, and legacy. Whether you prefer to relax in a historic hacienda or immerse yourself in the serenity of a cenote lodge, these accommodations may enhance your entire travel experience and help you build lasting memories of your stay in Merida.

CHAPTER THREE

Merida's Culinary Delights

Traditional Yucatecan Cuisine

Traditional Yucatecan cuisine is a delectable and tasty combination of Mayan, Spanish, and Lebanese influences that results in a one-of-a-kind gastronomic experience. The cuisine of the Yucatan Peninsula, which includes Merida, is recognized for its rich use of indigenous products, powerful spices, and unique cooking methods. Here are some must-try Yucatecan meals and specialties:

Cochinita Pibil: A popular Yucatecan meal, cochinita pibil is slow-roasted, marinated pork cooked in banana leaves with achiote (annatto) paste and sour orange juice. It's often accompanied with pickled onions and tortillas.

Poc Chuc: Another famous pig dish, poc chuc consists of thinly sliced grilled pork marinated in a combination of spices and sour orange juice. It's often accompanied with black beans, tortillas, and a light tomato-onion-cilantro salsa.

Salbutes and Panuchos are two must-try Yucatecan antojitos (snacks). Salbutes are little fried tortillas with shredded turkey, pickled onions, and avocado on top. Panuchos are identical to panuchos, except they feature a layer of refried black beans within the tortilla before being topped with the same components.

Sopa de Lima: A tangy and warming soup prepared with shredded chicken, lime, and crunchy tortilla strips.

Relleno Negro: A savory chicken or turkey meal cooked in a dark, rich sauce composed with charred chiles, spices, and ground baked tortillas.

Huevos Motuleos: A tasty breakfast meal that consists of fried eggs served on tortillas with black beans, ham, peas, plantains, and tomato sauce.

Queso Relleno: This Yucatan delicacy is a huge Edam cheese packed with minced pig, raisins, olives, and capers and served in a thick tomato sauce.

Marquesitas: Marquesitas are thin, crispy folded crepes filled with shredded Edam cheese and toppings such as Nutella, dulce de leche, or jam.

Papadzules: These folded tortillas filled with hard-boiled eggs and topped with pumpkin seed sauce are a Yucatecan favorite.

Pollo Pibil: Pollo pibil is marinated chicken cooked in banana leaves with achiote paste and citrus liquids, similar to cochinita pibil.

When in Merida, visit local markets and restaurants to sample these delectable Yucatecan specialties and learn about the region's rich culinary tradition. Good appetite!

Popular restaurants and grocery stores

Popular Merida Restaurants:

Yucatecan cuisine is served in **La Chaya Maya**. Location: Usually in the city core or near important attractions.

Yucatecan cuisine is served at **El Venadito.**

Location: Usually close to the Paseo de Montejo or the historic center.

Apoala Mexican Cuisine: Mexican Cuisine
Location: Typically located around the Paseo de Montejo or in the historic center.

Ku'uk's cuisine is modern Mexican.
Location: Typically found on the Paseo de Montejo or in wealthy communities.

Manjar Blanco: Yucatecan cuisine
Location: Usually in the city center or around the Plaza Grande.

Cuisine: Various foreign and Yucatecan meals are available at Mercado 60.
Location: In the city center, near the Plaza Grande.

Yucatecan cuisine is served at **El Trapiche**.

Location: Typically located in the city center or historic area.

Oliva Kitchen & Bar serves Mediterranean and Yucatecan fusion cuisine.

Location: Typically located on the Paseo de Montejo or historic district.

Merida's Food Markets

Market of Lucas de Galvez (Mercado de Lucas de Galvez): Calle 65, Centro, Merida, Yucatan.

A lively market selling fresh fruit, meats, fish, and traditional Yucatecan spices.

San Benito Market (Mercado San Benito): Centro, Calle 50-A x 63, Merida, Yucatan.

A bustling market with fresh fruits and vegetables, spices, and a variety of local cuisines and snacks.

The Santiago Market (Mercado de Santiago) is located at Calle 57 x 70 in Santiago, Merida, Yucatan.

A typical seafood, fresh vegetable, and regional specialty market.

The Santa Ana Market (Mercado de Santa Ana) is located at Calle 47 x 60 in Santa Ana, Merida, Yucatan.

A lovely market with a variety of food vendors serving Yucatecan cuisine as well as foreign delicacies.

It is pretty simple to go to these eateries and marketplaces. Taxis are commonly accessible in Merida and are a handy way to get about. Furthermore, many prominent restaurants and food markets are situated in or near the city center, making them conveniently accessible by foot or public transit.

Street Food and Must-Try Dishes

Merida's street food culture is dynamic and provides a delectable selection of delectable delicacies. Here are some must-try street snacks and regional specialties to sample during your visit:

Marquesitas are thin, crispy folded crepes filled with shredded Edam cheese and other toppings such as Nutella, dulce de leche, or jam. A popular treat offered at street food vendors.

Salbutes and Panuchos: Salbutes are little fried tortillas with shredded turkey, pickled onions, and avocado on top. Panuchos are identical to panuchos, except they feature a layer of refried black beans within the tortilla before being topped with the same components.

Tamales Colados: Made from masa dough and filled with chicken, pig, or beans, these tamales have a silky texture. Served with tomato sauce on the side.

Marinated Pork Tacos (Cochinita Pibil): Slow-roasted marinated pork wrapped in soft tortillas and served with pickled onions and habanero salsa.

Rolled tortillas stuffed with hard-boiled eggs and topped with a pumpkin seed sauce.

Pan de Cazón: Tortilla layers with shredded dogfish fish cooked in a tomato and pepper sauce.

Relleno Negro: Relleno Negro is a black, rich sauce prepared with charred chiles, spices, and ground baked tortillas.

Tacos de Longaniza: Tacos loaded with spicy, delicious longaniza sausage.

Esquites: A famous street food snack prepared with cooked corn kernels, mayonnaise, cheese, chili powder, and lime juice.

Raspados are shaved ice snacks flavored with syrups such as tamarind, mango, and strawberry.

Look for busy neighborhood markets, food kiosks, and street sellers while sampling Merida's street cuisine. Mercado 60, Mercado de Lucas de Galvez, and other tianguis (temporary street markets) that come up in different districts are some of the greatest venues to sample street cuisine.

To locate the most genuine and excellent food, seek vendors with clean and well-maintained booths and follow the locals' example. Street food sampling is not only a gastronomic experience, but also an opportunity to immerse yourself in Merida's lively and savory culture.

CHAPTER FOUR

Exploring Merida

Overview of Merida's History and Culture

Merida, Mexico's lively capital of the Yucatan Peninsula, has a rich history and a diversified cultural heritage. Here's a quick rundown of Merida's history and culture:

History:

Pre-Colonial Period: The Maya civilisation first settled in what is now Merida. The name "Merida" is a combination of the Spanish city of the same name and the Mayan word "T'Hó," which means "place of five hills."

Spanish Conquest: Merida was established in 1542 by Spanish conqueror Francisco de Montejo, making it one of the Americas' oldest continually inhabited towns. The settlement was constructed atop the remains of T'Hó, a Maya metropolis.

Colonial Period: During the colonial period, Merida prospered, and its historic center still displays stunning Spanish colonial architecture. The Spanish influence may be seen in the layout of the city, churches, and plazas.

The henequen (sisal) industry drove an economic boom in Merida in the late nineteenth and early twentieth century. Henequen was used to create ropes and other items, which brought the city enormous prosperity.

Yucatan Caste War: In the mid-nineteenth century, Merida and the Yucatan Peninsula saw the Caste War, an uprising of indigenous Mayans against the ruling elite. The conflict had a tremendous influence on the history and culture of the area.

Culture:

Mayan past: The cultural identity of Merida is heavily based in its Mayan past. Mayan influences may be seen in the local population's language, art, food, and cultural traditions.

Merida is recognized for its lively festivals and customs, which often combine Mayan and Spanish aspects. Hanal Pixan (Day of the Dead) celebrations and the Vaqueria dance highlight the city's cultural diversity.

Music and Dance: Traditional Yucatecan music and dance are important components of the city's cultural expression. A colorful dance performed during holidays, the Jarana, is a symbol of Yucatecan identity.

Gastronomy: Yucatecan cuisine is well-known for its distinctive tastes and ingredients. Cochinita pibil, papadzules, and panuchos are examples of Mayan, Spanish, and Lebanese culinary influences.

Art & Handicrafts: Merida is a creative hotspot, with several galleries, art centers, and craft fairs showing the work of local artists and craftsmen.

Meridanos are noted for their generosity and kindness toward guests, making it a pleasant location for travelers from all over the globe.

Merida today:

Economic hub: Merida has grown into a significant economic hub on the Yucatan Peninsula, drawing investments in a variety of sectors like as technology, manufacturing, and tourism.

Education and Research: The city is home to a number of universities and research organizations, which contribute to the region's intellectual and educational growth.

Tourism: Merida is a famous tourist destination due to its rich history, cultural offers, and closeness to ancient sites and natural beauties. Ancient ruins, cenotes, and colonial sites may all be explored by visitors.

history Preservation: The well-preserved colonial buildings, museums, and cultural organizations demonstrate efforts to conserve Merida's historical and architectural history.

Spanish and Mayan languages are extensively spoken in Merida, reflecting the city's varied culture. The Mayan language and customs are still an important element of the local culture.

Art & Creativity: Merida's art scene is thriving, with numerous artists and creatives adding to the city's cultural environment. Art exhibitions, galleries, and cultural events may be found all across the city.

Culinary Capital: Merida has acquired the title of Mexico's culinary capital. The city's restaurants and street food offerings highlight the finest of Yucatecan cuisine, drawing foodies from all around.

Religious and Spiritual legacy: The religious legacy of the city may be seen in its ancient churches and religious festivals, which merge Catholicism with pre-Hispanic beliefs and practices.

Warm Community: The people of Merida are recognized for their strong sense of identification and pride in their city. The Meridanos, or natives, are pleasant and ready to share their culture with guests.

Despite its modernization, Merida maintains a strong connection to its heritage. The blend of ancient Mayan legacy, Spanish colonial influence, and modern inventiveness in the city results in a lively and captivating destination. Visitors to Merida can enjoy a one-of-a-kind and enlightening experience, immersed in a city that honors its history while looking forward to the possibilities of the future. You will definitely leave with fond memories of this picturesque city in the center of the Yucatan Peninsula as you tour its ancient monuments, engage with people, and enjoy in its lively culture.

Today, Merida is a thriving city that honors its historical and cultural traditions while also emerging into a contemporary center of art, cuisine, and tourism. Visitors may learn about the city's intriguing history, enjoy its dynamic present, and see the city's ever-changing cultural scene.

Top Tourist Attractions

Paseo de Montejo

Paseo de Montejo is one of Merida's most famous and picturesque streets. It is well-known for its magnificent architecture, old homes, and tree-lined boulevards. Here's a rundown of Paseo de Montejo:

History:

The Paseo de Montejo was built in the late nineteenth century amid Merida's henequen boom. Its design was influenced by the beauty of Paris's Champs-Élysées, and construction started in 1888.

Francisco de Montejo, the Spanish conqueror who built Merida, was honored with the avenue's name. It was designed to be a great promenade for the rich elite, with sumptuous homes and European-style structures flanking its way.

The henequen boom brought considerable riches to Merida, and many henequen plantation owners constructed opulent houses along Paseo de Montejo to show off their wealth and success.

Architecture:

The architecture in Paseo de Montejo is a mix of French, Italian, and Moorish elements. The avenue's mansions and buildings include beautiful façade, exquisite wrought iron balconies, and stunning sculptures.

The Palacio Canton, which now houses the Regional Museum of Anthropology, and the twin homes known as "Los Palacios," which today serve as cultural institutions and museums, are two of the most notable structures.

Monuments and landmarks:

The Monument to the Homeland (Monumento a la Patria) is located on Paseo de Montejo and Calle 47. It is a magnificent white marble monument that commemorates Mexico's history and independence.

The Remate de Paseo de Montejo is a circular park at the northern end of the road that includes a reproduction of the "La Rotonde de l'Appel" in Paris.

Activities and Events:

Throughout the year, Paseo de Montejo holds a variety of cultural events, art exhibits, and festivals. During holidays and festivals, it serves as a focal point for huge parades and festivities. Locals and visitors alike love strolling along the road, taking in the surroundings and admiring the old buildings. Along the avenue, there are several cafés, restaurants, and boutiques.

Paseo de Montejo is a street in Merida, Yucatan, Mexico. It is roughly 5 kilometers (3.1 miles) long and goes north to south. The boulevard begins in the south at the Monument to the Homeland (Monumento a la Patria) and finishes in the north at the Remate de Paseo de Montejo, a circular park.

Because Paseo de Montejo is one of Merida's major thoroughfares, getting there is simple. Here are some frequent routes to Paseo de Montejo:

If you are in Merida's historic center, you may stroll or take a short cab journey to Paseo de Montejo. The avenue is just a few blocks west of the Plaza Grande (Main Square).

Merida has a well-developed public transportation system, which includes buses and combis (minivans). Many bus lines run through or near Paseo de Montejo, making it accessible from all across the city.

By Private Vehicle: If you own or hire a vehicle, you can simply get to Paseo de Montejo by driving to the avenue. The avenue is well-marked, and there are plenty of parking places available.

If you are staying in the city center or close by, try walking or cycling to Paseo de Montejo. It's a fun and relaxing way to explore the road and its surrounds.

Once reaching Paseo de Montejo, you may take a leisurely walk down the tree-lined boulevard, appreciate the stunning architecture, and explore the many sites and cultural institutes. Don't forget to soak in the beauty and history of Merida's famed Paseo de Montejo by stopping at the Monument to the Homeland and the Remate de Paseo de Montejo.

Paseo de Montejo is still a symbol of Merida's glorious history and a testimony to the city's rich cultural legacy today. It is a must-see for anybody visiting Merida, affording a look into the city's wealthy past as well as an amazing experience in this exquisite and historic boulevard.

Plaza Grande and the Cathedral of San Ildefonso

Plaza Grande, often known as the Zocalo, is the main plaza and core of Merida's historic center. It is a popular meeting spot for both residents and visitors, and it is bordered by some of the city's most important structures, including the Cathedral of San Ildefonso.

The Plaza Grande:

The Plaza Grande is situated in the historic center of Merida, near the confluence of Calle 60 and Calle 61. It is a major landmark in the city and is readily accessible.

The area is surrounded by colonial-style buildings that contain government offices and cultural organizations. These historic monuments include the Palacio de Gobierno (Government Palace) and Casa de Montejo (Montejo's House).

The Plaza Grande is a bustling hive of activity. Visitors may stroll around the nicely planted gardens and relax on the covered seats. Throughout the year, the plaza offers a variety of events, concerts, and cultural activities.

The Plaza Grande, Merida's heart, is culturally and historically significant, embodying the city's history and present. It serves as a focal point for festivities, festivals, and municipal events, and it is an important component of Merida's identity.

San Ildefonso Cathedral:

The Cathedral of San Ildefonso, which faces the Plaza Grande and dominates the city skyline with its twin towers, is located on the east side of the plaza.

The Cathedral of San Ildefonso is one of the Americas' oldest cathedrals. Construction on the site of a previous Mayan temple started in the

16th century. In the 18th century, the cathedral was finished.

The cathedral was built in the Spanish Renaissance style, with some Baroque features thrown in for good measure. Its front is adorned with elaborate carvings and sculptures, while the inside is filled with gorgeous altars, religious art, and historical antiques.

Religious and cultural significance: The Cathedral of San Ildefonso is Merida's main Catholic church. It serves as a vital spiritual focus for the community as well as a notable historical site that symbolizes the city's colonial origins.

The cathedral serves as a focal point for religious and cultural activities. Major religious celebrations and processions often start or end in the Plaza Grande and the cathedral.

Anyone visiting Merida should go to Plaza Grande and the Cathedral of San Ildefonso. It provides visitors with a view into the city's rich history, architectural splendor, and cultural legacy, making it a remarkable and rewarding experience.

Merida's Mayan World Museum

The Mayan World Museum (Museo del Mundo Maya) in Merida, Mexico, is a remarkable institution devoted to the Mayan civilization's rich cultural history. It displays relics, artworks, and exhibitions that provide light on the ancient and modern Mayan worlds. Here's a rundown of the museum:

Location:

The Mayan World Museum is situated on the outskirts of Merida, next to the Periferico highway. Calle 60, No. 299 E, Unidad Revolución, Merida, Yucatán, Mexico.

Collections and Exhibits:

The museum's displays span a wide range of Mayan civilization-related themes, from archaeology and history to art, language, and everyday life.

Ancient items: The museum has a substantial collection of archaeological items going back to different eras of Mayan history, including as pottery, sculptures, tools, and ceramics.

Ethnographic Exhibits: There are exhibitions devoted to modern Mayan communities, highlighting their rituals, traditions, and ways of life.

Interactive and multimedia exhibitions provide visitors with an immersive experience by mixing conventional exhibits with new technologies to engage and educate.

Architecture:

The ceiba tree, which bears tremendous symbolic value in Mayan cosmology, inspired the remarkable contemporary architectural style of the Mayan World Museum. The construction of the building resembles the shape of this holy tree, representing the museum's emphasis on Mayan culture and history.

Facilities:

The museum has guided tours, audio guides in many languages, a gift store, and a café.

Beautiful gardens and green areas surround the grounds, giving a comfortable atmosphere for guests to relax and enjoy the natural splendor.

Academic Programs:

The Mayan World Museum conducts educational programs, seminars, and cultural events to increase local and visitor understanding and appreciation of Mayan culture and history.

Visiting the Mayan World Museum is an excellent way to learn more about the Mayan civilization's astounding accomplishments and to develop a better appreciation of its legacy. It is a wonderful experience for history buffs, culture buffs, and everyone interested in the intriguing world of the ancient Maya.

Archaeological Site of Dzibilchaltun

Dzibilchaltun is a notable archaeological site in Yucatan, Mexico, about north of Merida. It is one of the region's most ancient Mayan towns, providing tourists with a look into the intriguing history and architecture of the ancient Maya culture. The following is a summary of the Dzibilchaltun Archaeological Site:

Location:

Dzibilchaltun is located around 15 kilometers (9 miles) north of Merida, making it an ideal day excursion from the city.

Historical Importance:

The history of Dzibilchaltun extends back over 2,000 years, with evidence of continuous habitation from the Preclassic through the Postclassic periods.

The site was a vital regional trading and agricultural hub, prospering because to its advantageous placement near coastal trade routes and cenotes (natural sinkholes containing fresh water).

The following are the main attractions:

The Temple of the Seven Dolls: This distinctive pyramid is called after seven miniature clay dolls discovered during excavations within the temple. During the spring and autumn equinoxes, it coincides with the rising sun, producing a spectacular natural phenomena.

The Xlacah Cenote: Dzibilchaltun is a public cenote where visitors may swim in crystal-clear waters and cool off in the tropical warmth of the Yucatan.

The Museum: The on-site museum displays archaeological objects and finds, offering vital context and insights into the site's past.

Activities for Cultural and Recreation:
Cultural events and activities are held at Dzibilchaltun, particularly around the equinoxes, when the Temple of the Seven Dolls aligns with the sun. These events draw both residents and visitors looking for one-of-a-kind experiences.

Visitors may wander around the site and see the historic sacbeob (Mayan causeways) that linked various parts of the city.

Visitor Services:

To improve the tourist experience, the facility provides visitor amenities such as bathrooms, shaded places, and educational panels. Local merchants often offer handicrafts and souvenirs, allowing tourists to support local craftspeople.

Dzibilchaltun exploration is a remarkable voyage back in time, where visitors may marvel at the spectacular architectural creations and immerse themselves in the enthralling Maya history. Because of its closeness to Merida, Dzibilchaltun is a must-see archaeological site for visitors interested in learning about the Yucatan Peninsula's rich cultural legacy.

Yucatan Haciendas

Yucatan's haciendas are ancient estates that have played an important part in the region's history, economics, and cultural legacy. These magnificent estates were originally agricultural production hubs, especially for henequen (sisal), and served as sumptuous mansions for affluent landowners throughout the colonial and post-colonial centuries. Many of these haciendas have been refurbished and repurposed into hotels, museums, or event spaces, enabling tourists to relive Yucatan's magnificence. Here's a rundown of Yucatan's haciendas:

History and Goal:
During the Spanish colonial era, vast land concessions were handed to Spanish immigrants, giving rise to the haciendas. These estates were mostly utilized for agricultural production, with henequen being the most

important cash crop in the late nineteenth and early twentieth century.

Henequen, a fiber collected from agave plants, was in high demand for ropes and other items across the globe, resulting in a henequen boom that brought immense prosperity to Yucatan.

The affluent landowners erected stunning hacienda constructions that blended European and native architectural styles to create one-of-a-kind and gorgeous structures.

Architecture and Design:

Large colonial-style residences with extensive courtyards and gardens are characteristic of haciendas.

They often feature beautiful facades, lofty ceilings, multicolored tiles, and wrought-iron accents, expressing their owners' wealth and splendor.

For henequen production, many haciendas contain enormous cisterns, equipment rooms, and processing spaces.

On occasion, chapels or churches might be seen on the grounds, showing the religious impact on everyday life.

Tourism and restoration:

The henequen business decreased over time, causing many haciendas to be abandoned or fall into ruin. Some, on the other hand, have been rehabilitated and turned into cultural institutions, boutique hotels, restaurants, and museums.

Several haciendas now provide guided tours, allowing tourists to learn about Yucatan's history, cultural value, and the henequen manufacturing process.

Staying at a hacienda hotel offers a one-of-a-kind and immersive experience, enabling visitors to appreciate the grandeur of the past while still enjoying contemporary conveniences.

Haciendas of note:

<u>Hacienda Sotuta de Peon:</u> This renowned restored hacienda near Merida offers tours and an authentic experience in henequen cultivation.

<u>Hacienda Temozon Sur:</u> This hacienda, now a luxury hotel, has been tastefully renovated and provides a look into the region's history and culture.

<u>Hacienda San Jose Cholul:</u> This renovated hacienda has been transformed into a boutique hotel, providing visitors with a beautiful and historical setting.

Visiting Yucatan's haciendas is a once-in-a-lifetime chance to go back in time, learn about the region's intriguing history, and appreciate the cultural legacy of this charming corner of Mexico.

Hidden Gems and Off-the-Beaten-Path Spots

While Merida has well-known attractions, it also has several hidden jewels and off-the-beaten-path locations that provide unique experiences. Here are a few worth investigating:

Yaxcopoil Hacienda:
The town is roughly 40 kilometers (25 miles) south of Merida.

How to go There: To go to Hacienda Yaxcopoil, use a cab or hire a vehicle. A well-preserved hacienda with a museum and stunning gardens makes for an excellent day excursion.

The Xbatun Cenote:
Location: It is around 40 kilometers (25 miles) southwest of Merida.

Here's how to get there: Consider taking a cab or renting a vehicle to go to Cenote Xbatun. Away from the tourists, this cenote provides a calm location for swimming and relaxation.

Mayan Archaeological Site of Uxmal:
Location: It is about 78 kilometers (48 miles) south of Merida.
Here's how to get there: To get to the Uxmal Ruins, you may join a guided tour, hire a vehicle, or utilize public transit. These

well-preserved Mayan ruins are a UNESCO World Heritage Site and provide a more tranquil experience than the more well-known Chichen Itza.

Tahdzibichén Hacienda San Antonio:

The town is around 60 kilometers (37 miles) southeast of Merida.

Here's how to get there: To visit this gorgeous restored hacienda, which now acts as a hotel and cultural center, take a cab or hire a vehicle.

Kankirixche Cenote:

Location: It is about 43 kilometers (27 miles) southeast of Merida.

Here's how to get there: Consider taking a cab or renting a vehicle to go to Cenote Kankirixche. Because to its cave formations and stalactites, this cenote provides a one-of-a-kind experience.

Biosphere Reserve of Celestun:

Location: It is around 95 kilometers (59 miles) west of Merida.

Here's how to get there: To get to Celestun, you may join a guided trip, hire a vehicle, or utilize public transit. This wildlife refuge, which includes pink flamingos, provides boat rides through the mangroves and lagoons.

The Hubiku Cenote:

The town is roughly 150 kilometers (93 miles) east of Merida.

Here's how to get there: Consider taking a cab or joining a guided tour to go to Cenote Hubiku. This cenote is nestled in a beautiful environment and provides a relaxing swim in its turquoise waters.

When visiting these off-the-beaten-path locations, it's essential to organize your transportation ahead of time, whether by booking a cab, renting a vehicle, or participating in guided excursions. To guarantee a memorable and comfortable trip, always check for current information and safety requirements before discovering these hidden jewels.

Natural Reserves and Parks

The Santa Ana Park:

Location: Near the Paseo de Montejo and the Plaza Grande in Merida's historic center.

If you are staying in the city center, you can easily get to Parque de Santa Ana by foot or by cab.

What to Do: This attractive park is ideal for relaxing, people-watching, and enjoying local street cuisine. Cultural events, concerts, and art exhibits are often held here.

Parque Centenario is located in the heart of Merida, near the Santiago Market.

How to Get There: The Parque Centenario is a short walk from the Plaza Grande and other significant city sites.

What to Do: The park has lovely gardens, a playground, and chairs where you can relax and take in the scenery. It's a great place for a walk or a picnic.

Cuxtal Ecological Reserve (Cuxtal Ecological Reserve):

Location: Located southwest of Merida, it encompasses a significant tract of protected natural terrain.

Here's how to get there: Consider taking a guided tour or booking a cab or private transportation to explore Cuxtal Ecological Reserve.

What to Do: Hiking routes, birding possibilities, and the opportunity to explore the region's unique flora and wildlife are all available at the reserve. It's an excellent destination for nature lovers and eco-tourists.

El Corchito Ecological Reserve is located in Progreso, about 36 kilometers (22 miles) north of Merida.

Here's how to get there: To go to El Corchito, take a bus or cab from Merida to Progreso and then a boat to the reserve.

What to Do: El Corchito is a group of freshwater cenotes that are ideal for swimming and cooling off in the Yucatan heat. The reserve is also a great place to go bird watching and get away from the city.

Ria Celestun Biosphere Reserve is located around 95 kilometers (59 miles) west of Merida, near the town of Celestun.

Here's how to get there: Consider taking a guided tour of the Celestun Biosphere Reserve or hiring a vehicle to go to the seaside hamlet of Celestun.

What to Do: The reserve is home to flocks of pink flamingos, and boat cruises through the mangroves allow you to see the plentiful birds and other animals.

Respect the natural environment and obey any instructions given by local authorities while visiting these parks and natural reserves in order to conserve these valuable ecosystems for future generations to enjoy. Before traveling, always check for latest information and safety requirements, and consider hiring local guides for a more meaningful trip.

CHAPTER FIVE

Shopping in Merida

Handicrafts and Souvenirs

Merida has a wide variety of handicrafts and souvenirs that highlight the region's rich cultural history and creative traditions. Here are some popular artisan and souvenir shops in Merida:

Location: Calle 65 and Calle 56, Centro, Merida.

How to Get There: Mercado Lucas de Galvez is located in the city center, close to the Plaza Grande and other prominent attractions.

What to Buy: The market sells a broad range of traditional Yucatecan handicrafts, such as embroidered fabrics, hammocks, handcrafted ceramics, colorful handwoven baskets, and traditional Yucatecan clothes.

Mercado de Artesanias: Calle 63, between Calle 64 and Calle 62 in Centro, Merida.

How to Get There: The Mercado de Artesanias is likewise centrally placed and can be accessed on foot or by cab from the city's major regions.

What to Buy: This market focuses on regional handicrafts, and you'll discover a wide range of traditional crafts here, including wooden carvings, leather products, and silver jewelry.

Hacienda Montecristo lies 40 kilometers (25 miles) northwest of Merida, near the town of Progreso.

How to Get There: You may join a guided tour or hire a vehicle for a day excursion from Merida to visit Hacienda Montecristo.

What to Buy: The hacienda offers a craft market where local craftsmen sell their goods like as textiles, embroidered apparel, and handmade accessories.

Bazar Garcia Rejon is located on Calle 57 in Centro, Merida, between Calle 60 and Calle 58.

How to Get There: Because Bazar Garcia Rejon is in the city center, it is conveniently accessible from many spots across Merida.

What to Buy: This market is well-known for its souvenirs, which include postcards, keychains, magnets, and other little memories that make ideal presents for friends and family.

Galeria La Eskalera is located on Calle 70 #474, Centro, Merida.

How to Get There: Galeria La Eskalera is conveniently placed near the Plaza Grande and other main attractions.

What to Buy: This gallery has a carefully chosen variety of high-quality crafts, modern art, and handcrafted jewelry produced by local artists and craftsmen.

When shopping at local markets, remember to haggle and negotiate pricing to obtain the greatest rates on your products. Shopping for handicrafts and souvenirs in Merida allows you to not only bring home beautiful and meaningful products, but also to support local craftsmen and the preservation of the region's cultural legacy.

Markets and shopping districts

Merida has a number of local markets and retail areas where you can discover a wide selection of things ranging from fresh fruit to handcrafted crafts. Here are some popular ones, along with directions:

Mercado de Santiago is located on Calle 70 and Calle 57 in Merida's Centro.

How to Get There: The Mercado de Santiago is located in the Santiago district, a short distance from the Plaza Grande.

Santa Ana Mercado: Calle 47 and Calle 60, Centro, Merida.

How to Get There: The Mercado de Santa Ana is conveniently situated near the Paseo de Montejo and the Plaza Grande, making it easy to reach on foot.

San Benito Market: Calle 73 and Calle 50, Centro, Merida.

How to Get There: The Mercado de San Benito lies in the heart of the city, near the Plaza Grande and other significant attractions.

Paseo de Montejo is a great roadway that runs from the Monument to the Homeland in the south to the Remate de Paseo de Montejo in the north.

Here's how to get there: The Paseo de Montejo is a short walk from the city center. To go to different spots along the route, you may either use a cab or public transit.

Calle 60 (Calle Montejo): Calle 60 is an important roadway that runs through the heart of Merida's historic district.

Here's how to get there: Calle 60 is a short walk from the Plaza Grande and other major city attractions.

Plaza Galerias is located on Calle 60 and Calle 35 in the Fraccionamiento Altabrisa neighborhood of Merida.

Here's how to get there: Plaza Galerias is a contemporary retail complex in the city's northwestern outskirts. To get to the mall from the city center, you may use a cab or public transit.

Whether you're searching for fresh vegetables, local crafts, apparel, or souvenirs, these markets and retail areas provide a great shopping experience. Exploring these dynamic retail districts will not only expose you to local culture but will also allow you to support local merchants and artists.

CHAPTER SIX

Nightlife and Entertainment

Bars, Clubs, and Live Music Venues

Merida's nightlife includes a variety of exciting pubs, clubs, and live music places where you may spend an enjoyable evening. Here are a few popular places to enjoy the city's nightlife and entertainment:

Cantina La Negrita:
The address is Calle 62 #426-A, Centro, Merida.
La Negrita Cantina is a well-known and historic tavern in the centre of the city. It provides a large variety of traditional Yucatecan beverages as well as live music, resulting in a vibrant and pleasurable ambiance.

Mezcaleria Fundación:

The address is Calle 55 #533, Centro, Merida.

This hip mezcal bar has a large selection of mezcal and creative drinks. It's a terrific spot to savour the flavors of Mexico's cherished spirit in a contemporary and trendy setting.

The Mala Vida Bar:

Calle 21 #103-C, Colonia Mexico, Merida, Mexico.

Mala Vida Bar is a renowned nightlife destination noted for its vibrant ambiance, live music, and delicious drinks. It often has live bands and DJs, making it popular with both residents and visitors.

Latino Pea del Sol:

The address is Calle 64 #442, Centro, Merida.

About La Pea del Sol Latino: La Pea del Sol Latino is a lively bar and cultural center that hosts live music, dance performances, and other creative activities. It's a terrific location to become involved in the local cultural scene.

Merida Casino Life:

Plaza Galerias, Avenida Itzaes, Fraccionamiento Altabrisa, Merida.

Casino Life provides slot machines, table games, and live entertainment in a contemporary casino atmosphere for individuals who appreciate gambling and enjoyment.

Centro La Bierhaus:

The address is Calle 62 #495-A, Centro, Merida.

La Bierhaus is a German-style tavern with an exceptional assortment of craft beers from both local and foreign brewers. It's a relaxing place to unwind and interact with friends.

The Mayan Pub:

Location: Centro, Calle 70 #480-A, Merida.

About: The Mayan Pub has a vibrant environment with live music, which includes traditional Yucatecan trova and other regional styles. It's an excellent location for discovering the local music scene.

It is important to note that the nighttime scene in Merida varies based on the day of the week and local events. To get the most of your nighttime experience in this dynamic city, check the timetables and prepare ahead of time. Respect the local culture and traditions while enjoying the nightlife responsibly.

Festivals and cultural events

Merida's cultural events and festivals reflect the city's robust tradition and creative community.

Here are some of the major cultural events and festivals held in Merida throughout the year:

Festival Internacional de la Cultura Maya (International Mayan Culture Festival): January
About: This well-known festival honors Mayan culture via a variety of activities like as traditional dance performances, art exhibits, music concerts, seminars, and conferences. It provides an interesting look at the ancient and modern Mayan heritage.

Carnaval de Merida (Merida Carnival):
Date(s): February or March (before to Lent)
The Carnaval de Merida is a bright and cheerful celebration that includes parades, music, dancing, and spectacular costumes. It's a lively festival with a distinct Yucatecan flavor.

Santa Semana (Holy Week):

Date: March or April (varies depending on the year)

Semana Santa is a major religious holiday in Merida, including processions, reenactments of biblical events, and ancient rites. For the local community, it is a time of introspection and devotion.

Noche Blanca: April, July, October, and December (many events throughout the year)

About: Noche Blanca is a cultural festival held multiple times a year in Merida, when art, music, dance, and performances fill the streets. Museums, galleries, and cultural institutions are open late and give free admission to exhibits and events.

Feria Yucatan Xmatkuil:

Dates: November-December (around the Christmas season)

This agricultural fair is one of Yucatan's most important events, including cattle shows, rodeos, carnival rides, local cuisine, live music, and cultural performances. It's a fun, family-friendly event.

Festival de las Animas (Souls Festival):

Date: Late October to early November (about around the Day of the Dead)

About: The Festival de las Animas commemorates Day of the Dead customs by gathering families to pay tribute to their lost loved ones. Throughout the city, altars, art displays, and cultural events are hosted.

Merida en Domingo (Sundays in Merida):

On every Sunday

On Sundays, Merida's downtown district becomes pedestrian-only, with numerous cultural events including as live music, dancing performances, art displays, and open-air marketplaces taking place. It's a great opportunity to take in the city's vibrant atmosphere.

These cultural events and festivals are an excellent way to learn about Merida's diverse traditions, arts, and customs. Check the particular dates of the events you want to attend while organizing your trip to avoid missing out on these colourful festivities.

CHAPTER SEVEN

Outdoor Activities and Adventure

Eco-Tours and Nature Excursions

Merida and its surrounding area provide a variety of outdoor activities and eco-tours that enable you to discover the Yucatan Peninsula's natural beauty and different ecosystems. Here are some popular eco-tours and nature excursions, as well as their locations and directions:

Celestun Biosphere Reserve is about 95 kilometers (59 miles) west of Merida, near the town of Celestun.

Here's how to get there: Consider taking a guided tour of the Celestun Biosphere Reserve or hiring a vehicle to go to the seaside hamlet of Celestun.

What to Do: The reserve is well-known for its pink flamingo colonies, and boat cruises through the mangroves allow you to see a variety of bird species, crocodiles, and other animals.

Cenote Cuzama is situated around 50 kilometers (31 miles) east of Merida, near the town of Cuzama.

Here's how to get there: To see Cenote Cuzama, you may join a guided trip or hire a vehicle in Cuzama.

What to Do: This cenote system provides a one-of-a-kind journey, with historic horse-drawn vehicles known as "trucks" transporting you to the cenotes hidden in the forest.

Sian Ka'an Biosphere Reserve:

Location: The Sian Ka'an Biosphere Reserve is situated in the state of Quintana Roo, roughly 300 kilometers (186 miles) south of Merida.

Here's how to get there: You may take a guided trip from Merida or hire a vehicle for a multi-day expedition to see Sian Ka'an.

What to Do: This large biosphere reserve is a UNESCO World Heritage Site, including marshes, beaches, and ancient Mayan ruins among its many landscapes. Birdwatching, snorkeling, and visiting old archaeological sites are also popular hobbies.

Cenote Xlacah is located around 40 kilometers (25 miles) southwest of Merida.

Here's how to get there: Consider taking a cab or renting a vehicle to go to Cenote Xlacah. It's a great place to swim and cool down in a natural cenote with cave structures.

Archaeological Sites of Uxmal and Kabah:

Location: Uxmal is around 78 kilometers (48 miles) south of Merida, while Kabah is about 90 kilometers (56 miles) away.

How to Get There: To explore Uxmal and Kabah, you may take guided excursions or hire a vehicle. Both locations provide a chance to see spectacular Mayan ruins in a more calm and less crowded atmosphere.

It is important to follow the rules established by tour operators while participating in eco-tours and environmental excursions in order to maintain the environment and respect the local flora and wildlife. Choose ethical and eco-friendly travel operators that value conservation and sustainability. These outdoor activities and excursions will definitely give you with amazing experiences and a stronger connection to the Yucatan Peninsula's natural marvels.

Water Sports and Beach Activities

Because of its gorgeous coastline along the Gulf of Mexico and the Caribbean Sea, the Yucatan Peninsula provides a range of water sports and beach activities. Here are some popular water sports and beach activities, as well as their locations and directions:

Progreso Beach: Progreso is a beach town around 36 kilometers (22 miles) north of Merida.

How to Get There: From Merida, take a bus or cab to Progreso. The travel takes around 30-45 minutes.

Swimming, jet skiing, paddleboarding, and beach volleyball are all available at Progreso Beach. Tours for fishing and boating are also available.

Sisal Beach: Sisal is a lovely fishing hamlet located around 55 kilometers (34 miles) northwest of Merida.

How to Get There: From Merida, you may take a bus or hire a vehicle to Sisal, which takes approximately an hour.

Sisal Beach is perfect for swimming and relaxation. It's a quiet and less busy beach, making it ideal for a relaxing beach day.

Holbox Island is situated off the northern coast of the Yucatan Peninsula and is accessible by boat from the town of Chiquila.

Here's how to get there: To get to Isla Holbox, take a bus or drive from Merida to Chiquila, then board a boat.

Water Sports: Isla Holbox is a water sports enthusiast's delight. To discover the rich marine life, you may do kiteboarding, windsurfing, paddleboarding, kayaking, and snorkeling.

Playa del Carmen is a prominent Riviera Maya beach resort located around 320 kilometers (199 miles) southeast of Merida.

How to go There: From Merida, the most convenient way to go to Playa del Carmen is to take a domestic flight or hire a vehicle for a road trip.

Water Sports: Scuba diving, snorkeling in the coral reefs, jet skiing, and parasailing are all available at Playa del Carmen.

Tulum Beach: Tulum is a seaside town about 330 kilometers (205 miles) southeast of Merida.

How to Get There: Take a domestic aircraft or hire a vehicle and drive to Tulum.

Water Sports: Tulum's beaches are known for their pristine seas, which make snorkeling, paddleboarding, and swimming in cenotes possible.

When participating in water sports and beach activities, be sure to follow any directions given by local guides or operators. While visiting these gorgeous coastal places, keep environmental protection in mind and preserve the marine life and ecosystems.

Day Trips and Excursions

Chichen Itza and Other Mayan Ruins
Celestun Biosphere Reserve

Chichen Itza: Chichen Itza is an ancient Mayan archaeological site on Mexico's Yucatan Peninsula. It is around 120 kilometers (75 miles) east of Merida and 200 kilometers (124 miles) west of Cancun.

How to Get There: To see Chichen Itza, you may join a guided tour, hire a private driver, or rent a vehicle from Merida. The road trip takes roughly 2 to 2.5 hours.

Chichen Itza is one of Mexico's most well-known and well-preserved Mayan ruins, designated as a UNESCO World Heritage Site and one of the New Seven Wonders of the World. The site was originally a significant

Mayan civilization center, with spectacular architectural marvels including the Pyramid of Kukulkan (El Castillo), the Temple of Warriors, the Great Ball Court, and the Sacred Cenote. The historical and cultural importance of Chichen Itza draws people from all over the globe.

Celestun Biosphere Reserve is situated on the northwest coast of the Yucatan Peninsula, about 95 kilometers (59 miles) west of Merida and roughly 350 kilometers (217 miles) west of Cancun.

How to Get There: From Merida, you may join a guided trip, hire a vehicle, or use public transit to Celestun. The road trip takes roughly 1.5 to 2 hours.

Celestun Biosphere Reserve is a RAMSAR site and a protected natural area recognized for its various habitats, which include estuaries, mangroves, wetlands, and sandy beaches. The reserve is home to a diverse range of animals, including flocks of pink flamingos that congregate in the area's small lagoons. Boat cruises through the mangroves may be taken to see the flamingos, as well as other bird species, crocodiles, and other marine life. The reserve is a paradise for nature enthusiasts, offering a tranquil and scenic respite from the hustle and bustle of the city.

Chichen Itza and Celestun Biosphere Reserve both provide amazing experiences. Chichen Itza offers a fascinating peek into the ancient Mayan civilization's architectural and astrological accomplishments, whilst Celestun enables you to interact with nature and see the beautiful landscapes and fauna of Yucatan. To get the most of your exploration, schedule your trips carefully and consider attending guided tours.

The Yellow City, Izamal

Izamal, sometimes known as the "Yellow City," is a lovely and ancient town on Mexico's Yucatan Peninsula. Here is some further information on Izamal:

Izamal is located roughly 72 kilometers (45 miles) east of Merida, the state capital of Yucatan.

The Yellow City: Izamal was given the moniker "the Yellow City" because of the bright yellow hue of many of its buildings. This one-of-a-kind feature lends the town a visually appealing and magical environment.

Izamal is historically and culturally noteworthy as one of the Yucatan's oldest continuously inhabited cities, having a history extending back to the Pre-Columbian Maya civilization. It was a significant sacred site devoted to Kinich Kak Moo, the Maya sun deity.

Convento de San Antonio de Padua: The Convento de San Antonio de Padua (Convent of San Antonio) is one of Izamal's most recognizable monuments. This massive Franciscan monastery was constructed on top of an old Maya pyramid, highlighting the fusion of Maya and Spanish colonial architecture. The convent's façade and walls are likewise painted in a bright yellow tint, adding to the town's distinct aspect.

Kinich Kak Moo Pyramid: The Kinich Kak Moo Pyramid, dedicated to the sun deity, is open to visitors in Izamal. The pyramid offers a fantastic view of the town's golden roofs and surrounding landscape.

Horse-Drawn Carriages and Cobblestone Streets: The town's tiny cobblestone streets and lack of contemporary traffic add to its lovely and serene ambience. Horse-drawn carriages are a popular way for visitors to experience Izamal's scenic streets and sights.

Izamal is well-known for its artisan goods, which include textiles, handwoven baskets, and delicately created jewelry. Visitors may discover a variety of souvenirs and one-of-a-kind items to take home as keepsakes of their stay.

The charm of Izamal is found not just in its bright color, but also in its rich history and cultural legacy. Its timeless elegance, friendly residents, and well-preserved colonial architecture make it an appealing location for those seeking a genuine Yucatecan experience.

Valladolid and Ek Balam:Valladolid and Ek Balam are two intriguing Yucatan Peninsula sites, each with its own distinct experiences and historical importance. Here's additional information about both locations:

Valladolid's location is roughly 160 kilometers (99 miles) east of Merida, making it reasonably accessible for a day trip or overnight stay. Valladolid is one of Mexico's Pueblos Magicos (Magic Towns), noted for its cultural and historical importance. The town, founded in 1543, combines Spanish colonial and Mayan characteristics.

The beautiful San Gervasio Cathedral (also known as the cathedral of San Servacio) is the highlight of Valladolid, a grand colonial-style cathedral with an exquisitely crafted façade and interior. The cathedral's center placement in the Zocalo, or main plaza, contributes to its majesty.

Cenote Zaci: Valladolid is also famous for its cenotes, with Cenote Zaci being one of the most well-known. This cenote is readily accessible and allows visitors to cool down in its crystal-clear waters while being surrounded by lush greenery and unique rock formations.

Valladolid is a good site to sample authentic Yucatecan food. Local dishes including cochinita pibil (slow-cooked pork), panuchos, and salbutes may be found at the town's cafés and street food sellers.

Ek Balam is situated in the middle of the Yucatan Peninsula, roughly 30 kilometers (19 miles) north of Valladolid.

Ek Balam is an archaeological site that was once a major Maya metropolis during the Classic Period. It has well-preserved monuments, such as the majestic El Torre pyramid, which rises around 30 meters (98 feet) tall and gives panoramic views from the summit. Other ceremonial buildings, ball courts, and an old sacbe (Maya causeway) network may be explored by visitors.

Stucco ornamentation: The elaborate stucco ornamentation seen on the main pyramid and surrounding buildings is one of the attractions of Ek Balam. The stucco work has intricate carvings and patterns that provide vital insights into Mayan creative expressions.

Natural Surroundings: Ek Balam is set inside a beautiful forest environment, which adds to the site's allure and adventure.

Valladolid and Ek Balam both provide unique insights into Mexico's rich history and cultural heritage. These two places give a well-rounded experience for tourists touring the Yucatan Peninsula, from experiencing colonial architecture and cenotes in Valladolid to diving into the ancient Maya culture at the Ek Balam ruins.

Photography Tips

Capturing the Best of Merida's Landscapes

Capturing the finest of Merida's sceneries requires an eye for beauty as well as a camera capable of capturing the breathtaking views. Here are some pointers to help you get the most out of your Merida landscape photography:

Golden Hour: Take advantage of the magnificent golden hour, which comes between the first hour after dawn and the last hour before sunset. This time of year, the soft, warm light accentuates the colors and textures of the landscapes, producing a great ambience for your images.

Wide-Angle Lens: To capture the immensity of Merida's landscapes, use a wide-angle lens. This lens lets you incorporate additional things in your frame, such as historic structures, beautiful parks, and expansive cityscapes.

Include Local aspects: To give your images a feeling of location and cultural identity, include aspects specific to Merida, such as colorful colonial buildings, Mayan-inspired architecture, and bustling street markets.

Experiment with Composition: To produce aesthetically interesting and dynamic images, experiment with various composition strategies such as the rule of thirds, leading lines, and framing.

Capture Reflections: Whether it's a cenote, a park fountain, or a historic structure beside a river, Merida's landscapes often incorporate bodies of water. Seek for chances to capture reflections, which add depth and intrigue to your photographs.

Explore the natural surroundings around Merida, such as the cenotes, the shoreline at Progreso, and the lush foliage in parks and reserves. These natural locations provide a variety of interesting topics for your photography.

Capture the sceneries of Merida at night, when the city comes alive with lights and a new mood. To produce breathtaking nightscapes, use a tripod to keep your camera stable and experiment with lengthy exposures.

Capture Local Life: Include people going about their daily lives, street sellers, and locals in your landscape shots. This adds a human aspect to your photographs while also telling a tale about the culture of the place.

Weather Considerations: Dress appropriately for the weather, since Merida can become extremely hot throughout the day. Stay hydrated and protect yourself and your equipment from the sun while shooting.

Take your time and enjoy the experience of capturing the beauty of Merida's landscapes. Take many photographs from various angles and viewpoints to ensure you have a wide range of alternatives when choosing the finest images to represent this bustling city.

Cultural Sensitivities Must Be Respected
When visiting a new area, such as Merida, Mexico, or any other destination, it is important to respect cultural sensitivity. Here are some

pointers to help you have a polite and enjoyable experience when visiting another culture:

Educate Yourself: Learn about the destination's local customs, traditions, and cultural norms. Understanding the local culture can help you negotiate encounters with sensitivity and respect.

Appropriate Dress: Respect the clothing standards of the area, particularly while visiting religious or sensitive places. In many locations, modest clothing is preferred, and shoulders and knees must be covered.

Learn a few simple words in the local language, such as greetings and thank-yous. The use of polite language demonstrates that you appreciate and respect the local culture.

Always request permission before photographing individuals, particularly in intimate or sensitive settings. Some cultures may consider having their images taken without their agreement to be invasive.

Be Aware of Your Gestures: Be aware of the diverse meanings of hand gestures in different cultures. Some benign gestures in one culture may be insulting in another.

Respect Personal Space: Respect personal space and avoid touching individuals without their consent, particularly in cultures where personal boundaries are valued.

Respect Religious Practices: When visiting religious locations, adhere to the norms and restrictions established by the location of worship. Show respect and avoid interfering with current rites or rituals.

Respect the Environment and Local Wildlife: Be aware of your environmental impact. Dispose of waste appropriately, prevent harming natural places, and promote environmentally friendly actions.

Be Patient and Open-Minded: When experiencing diverse cultural practices or traditions, be patient and open-minded. Accept the differences as a chance to learn and develop.

Choose to support local businesses, craftsmen, and cultural events to help the local economy and culture. This contributes to the preservation of traditional customs and ensures that tourism benefits the local community.

By being sensitive to cultural sensitivities, you not only demonstrate respect for the local culture, but you also contribute to a good and enriching travel experience for both yourself and the local population. It promotes cultural awareness and appreciation while fostering a closer connection with the area and its people.

CHAPTER EIGHT

Art and Culture Scene

Galleries and Art Exhibitions

Gran Museo del Mundo Maya (Great Maya World Museum):
Calle 60, #299E, Unidad Revolución, Merida.
About: This museum displays a large collection of Maya artifacts and art, allowing visitors to learn about the interesting history and culture of the Maya civilisation.

Galleria Mérida: Calle 64 #398A, Centro, Merida.
Galera Mérida is a contemporary art gallery that shows paintings, sculptures, and mixed media works by local and international artists.

Juan Gamboa Guzmán Pinacoteca: Calle 61 #524, Centro, Merida.

About: This art gallery displays a variety of historical and modern art works, allowing visitors to have a full understanding of Yucatan's cultural past.

Location of Luz en el Bolsillo: Calle 64A #454, Centro, Merida.

Luz en el Bolsillo is a cultural center and art space that conducts art exhibits, seminars, and cultural events to assist rising local artists.

Galleria Tres Pajaros: Calle 58 #488, Centro, Merida.

Galera Tres Pájaros focuses on folk and indigenous art, displaying traditional crafts as well as modern pieces influenced by Mexican culture.

Hennessy Art Forum's address is Calle 60 #465, Centro, Merida.

Hennessy Art Forum is a creative place that supports contemporary art and holds exhibits and cultural activities on a regular basis.

Plaza Grande Artisans may be found at Plaza Grande, Centro, Merida.

The Plaza Grande is a popular meeting spot with craftsmen and sellers offering homemade crafts, paintings, and Yucatecan cultural souvenirs.

El Laberinto Gallery is located in Calle 56 #426, Centro, Merida.

About: Galera El Laberinto exhibits a wide range of artworks by local and national artists, including paintings, sculptures, and photography.

Museo de Arte Popular de Yucatan (Yucatan Museum of Popular Art): Calle 50 #487, Centro, Merida.

This museum focuses on conserving and promoting Yucatecan folk art and traditional crafts, taking visitors on a cultural journey via the works of local artisans.

Exploring Merida's galleries and art exhibits will not only immerse you in the city's creative expression, but will also provide you with a better appreciation of the Yucatan's rich cultural legacy. Have fun on your artistic tour of the Yellow City!

Folklore and traditional performances

Traditional performances and folklore represent the region's history and different influences on Merida's cultural heritage. Here are some examples of traditional performances and folklore encounters in Merida:

Jarana Yucateca Dance: The Jarana Yucateca is a brilliant and colorful traditional dance that shows the Yucatan Peninsula's dynamic culture. The music is complemented by the sounds of guitars, violins, and harps, and the dancers wear extravagant costumes. Jarana Yucateca performances may be seen at cultural events, festivals, and traditional gatherings.

Vaqueria is a traditional dance that pays homage to the region's ranching history. Dancers wear traditional attire, such as an embroidered dress for ladies and a guayabera shirt for males. The dance is often accompanied by marimba music, which adds to the celebratory and joyous ambiance.

Yucatan Trova Serenade: Yucatan Trova is a popular folk music genre with lyrical lyrics and melodies. Serenades are nighttime performances by musicians in which they sing romantic and nostalgic melodies in public places or in front of residences. Serenades provide insight on the region's amorous customs.

Day of the Dead Hanal Pixan

Celebrations: Hanal Pixan is a traditional Mayan Day of the Dead festival. Families remember their lost loved ones with colorful altars, offerings, and traditional meals throughout this time. These spectacular and profound gatherings may be seen in cemeteries and public locations across Merida and the Yucatan.

Mayan Rituals and rites: Some communities on the Yucatan Peninsula continue to observe ancient Mayan rituals and rites, which give an intriguing glimpse into the region's pre-Hispanic history. During special events or arranged tours, you may be able to participate in or observe these rituals.

Traditional Theater and Storytelling: Local stories, historical events, and traditional tales are often included in traditional theater performances and storytelling gatherings. These shows are a fun and instructive way to learn about the region's folklore and cultural history.

Folkloric Ballet: Folkloric ballet ensembles in Merida offer lively and energetic dances that reflect Mexico's ethnic variety. These shows often incorporate dances from many parts of the nation, highlighting unique customs and costumes.

Look for cultural events, festivals, and local performances taking place during your vacation to Merida to enjoy these traditional performances and traditions. Consider visiting museums and cultural institutions that host exhibits and performances aimed at conserving and promoting the region's cultural legacy. Embracing these customs and folklore will give you a better understanding of Merida's distinct identity and creative expression.

Merida with Kids

Family-Friendly Attractions and Activities

Merida has a wide range of family-friendly attractions and activities for children of all ages. Here are some of the best locations to visit and activities to do in Merida with kids:

Animaya Interactive Zoo is located at Calle 60, Kilometer 14.5 in Merida.
Animaya is an interactive zoo that emphasizes teaching and conservation. Children may view and learn about a variety of animal species such as exotic birds, reptiles, and mammals. There are also playgrounds and picnic spaces in the zoo.

Gran Museo del Mundo Maya (Great Maya World Museum):
Calle 60, #299E, Unidad Revolución, Merida.

This museum is a great location for youngsters to learn about the Maya civilization's history and culture via interactive exhibits, artifacts, and multimedia displays.

EcoParque Animaya is located on the Carretera Xcunya-Dzoyaxche in Merida.

EcoParque Animaya provides outdoor activities and natural experiences for children. It has walking paths, playgrounds, and a petting zoo, allowing visitors to interact with nature.

Centenario Zoológico Park

Location: Calle 59 #598, Merida (Centennial Zoo).

The Centennial Zoo is a popular destination for families. It is home to a variety of creatures, including lions, elephants, and monkeys, and offers youngsters a fun and informative experience.

Location of Parque de Las Américas (Las Americas Park): Calle 60 x 89, Colonia Garca Ginerés, Merida.

About: With spacious playgrounds, walking routes, and green areas, this park is great for youngsters to run, play, and enjoy outdoor activities.

Acuaparque La Ceiba (La Ceiba Water Park): Carretera Mérida-Motul Kilometer 5.5, Merida.

About: La Ceiba Water Park has water slides, pools, and splash zones, making it ideal for a day of family fun and excitement.

Granja Animaya: Address: Circuito Colonias #202, Colonia Xoclán, Merida.

About Granja Animaya: Granja Animaya is a family-friendly farm where children can engage with farm animals, learn about agriculture, and ride tractors.

Calle 59 x 68, Colonia Centro, Merida; Parque de las Palapas *(Palapas Park).*

About Palapas Park: Palapas Park is a dynamic urban park with playgrounds, open spaces, and food sellers that provides a lively and pleasurable environment for families.

Plaza Sendero Mall can be found on Carretera Mérida-Progreso in Merida.

Plaza Sendero Mall offers a number of family-friendly activities, such as a cinema, a play area, and a choice of retail and eating options.

Exploration of Cenotes: Several cenotes on the Yucatan Peninsula, such as Cenote Zaci in Valladolid and Cenote Xlacah in Merida, provide a unique and exhilarating chance for children to swim in clear, freshwater sinkholes.

These family-friendly Merida attractions and activities guarantee that both children and adults have a memorable and pleasurable time exploring the city and its surrounds. Merida has something for everyone in the family, whether it's learning about history and environment or just having fun in parks and water parks.

Tips for Childcare and Safety

When coming to Merida with children, it is important to ensure their safety and well-being. Here are some childcare and safety reminders:

Keep a watchful check on your children at all times, particularly in busy situations or new locales. Avoid leaving children alone, even for a short time.

In case of an emergency, carry identification for your children, such as a copy of their passport or birth certificate.

Stay Hydrated: Because the weather in Merida may be hot and humid, make sure your children drink lots of water throughout the day.

Sun Protection: Keep your children safe from the sun's rays by administering sunscreen to them, equipping them with hats and sunglasses, and taking them out of the sun during peak hours.

Insect Repellent: Use insect repellent to protect yourself from mosquito bites, particularly if you want to spend time outside.

Be Wary of Food and drink: To prevent health problems, make sure your children eat safe and sanitary food and drink. Drink only bottled water and avoid eating raw or undercooked food.

Child-Friendly lodgings: Select family-friendly lodgings with childproofing features such as outlet covers and safety gates.

Seat Belts and automobile Seats: When traveling by automobile with children, always use seat belts and suitable car seats.

Familiarize yourself with local emergency numbers, including those for medical aid, police, and fire services.

When travelling about the city or going on a day excursion, use trustworthy transportation providers and drivers.

Allow your youngsters to relax and take pauses throughout touring to avoid tiredness.

Childcare Services: If you need childcare, enquire with your lodging about reputable providers or seek referrals from recognized sources.

Familiarize Yourself with the Area: Get to know the area surrounding your lodging, especially neighboring medical services and pharmacies.

Cultural Sensitivities: Teach your children about the local culture and traditions so that they can interact with respect and sensitivity.

By following these childcare and safety precautions, you can ensure that your children have a safe and pleasurable time while enjoying the delights of Merida and the Yucatan Peninsula.

CHAPTER NINE

Health and Wellness

Spas and Wellness Centers

Merida has a number of spas and wellness facilities where you may unwind, revitalize, and enjoy luxurious treatments. Here are a some of the prominent alternatives in the city:

Rosas & Xocolate Boutique Hotel + Spa is located at Paseo de Montejo #480 in Merida's Colonia Centro.

About: This premium boutique hotel has a well-known spa that offers a variety of services such as massages, facials, body scrubs, and hydrotherapy. The stylish and serene ambience of the spa is ideal for relaxation.

Location: Calle 19 S/N, Tablaje Catastral #565, Santa Rosa, Merida.

Ki'óol Spa is located inside the Hacienda Misné hotel and combines ancient Maya traditions with contemporary spa services. Natural substances and Mayan-inspired rituals are often used in treatments here.

Wayak Spa at Hacienda Xcanatn: Calle 20 S/N, Comisara Xcanatn, Merida.

The Wayak Spa at Hacienda Xcanatn is a tranquil retreat with an emphasis on holistic wellbeing. Massages, aromatherapy, and facial treatments are available, as is access to a steam room and Jacuzzi.

Location of the *Spa del Hotel Mansion Merida:* Calle 59 #498, Centro, Merida.

This spa, located inside the Hotel Mansion Merida, provides a variety of luxury services such as massages, body wraps, and facials. The historic environment contributes to the overall relaxing experience.

The Ku Spa at the Hyatt Regency Merida is located at Avenida Colón #344 in Merida. The Hyatt Regency Merida's Ku Spa offers a range of wellness treatments and amenities, including a fitness center and an outdoor pool. The spa's services are geared at relaxation and renewal.

Spa Fiesta Americana Mérida is located at Paseo de Montejo #451 in Merida's Colonia Centro.

About: The Spa Fiesta Americana provides massages, facials, and body treatments in a relaxing and modern setting. It's a great place to relax after a day of touring.

Holistika Mérida is located in Calle 33A #540A in Colonia México, Merida.

Holistika Mérida is a holistic wellness facility that provides a variety of therapeutic treatments, yoga courses, meditation sessions, and seminars centered on total well-being.

These spas and wellness facilities in Merida are ideal for unwinding and getting away from the hustle and bustle of the city. Whether you want a lavish spa experience or a holistic approach to wellbeing, there are several alternatives to suit your interests and requirements.

Retreats for Yoga and Meditation

Merida and its environs provide a peaceful and calm setting, making it a great location for yoga and meditation retreats. Here are some noteworthy retreat places and venues where you may start on a self-discovery and relaxing journey:

__Holistika Mérida__ is located in Calle 33A #540A in Colonia México, Merida.

Holistika Mérida is a holistic wellness facility that offers yoga and meditation retreats, as well as seminars and lectures on mindfulness and personal development.

__Casa Lunita__ is located in Telchac Puerto, Yucatan (about 1.5 hours from Merida).

Casa Lunita is a beachside yoga retreat facility that provides immersive experiences in a tranquil seaside location. Yoga, meditation, nutritious food, and beach trips are often included in retreats here.

__Perri's Yoga:__ Location: Various sites in and around Merida.

Yoga with Perri provides monthly yoga sessions and seminars in a variety of locations, including indoor studios and outdoor places, allowing for individualized practice and development.

T'aan Yoga Merida's address is Calle 55A #503B, Centro, Merida.

T'aan Yoga Merida is a yoga studio that provides a range of yoga, meditation, and holistic well-being programs, seminars, and retreats.

Location of ***Hacienda Chichen Resort & Yaxkin Spa:*** Carretera Mérida-Puerto Juárez Km 120, Chichen Itza, Yucatán.

This resort and spa, located near the historic Mayan ruins of Chichen Itza, offers yoga and meditation programs in gorgeous gardens and natural environs.

La Casa Surya Yoga & Wellness is located in Merida's San Ramón Norte neighborhood.

La Casa Surya is a health facility that offers yoga courses and retreats in a loving environment, with an emphasis on personal development and balance.

Location: Various places in and around Merida for ***Ikal Anah*** Retreats.

Ikal Anah provides yoga and meditation retreats that integrate inner discovery with cultural experiences such as archaeological site tours and absorption in local customs.

These yoga and meditation retreats in and around Merida are ideal for reconnecting with yourself, finding inner peace, and deepening your yoga practice. Whether you choose a tranquil beach environment or a lush jungle hideaway, the alternatives appeal to all tastes and give participants with a transforming experience.

CHAPTER TEN

Practical Information

Local Customs and Etiquette

When visiting Merida or any new place, it is essential to understand and respect local traditions and etiquette. Here are some helpful hints for navigating cultural customs and making a good impression:

Handshakes are a normal and courteous greeting when meeting someone for the first time. A loving embrace or a cheek kiss may be traditional in more casual circumstances, particularly among friends and relatives.

Use Polite Language: Show respect for others by using polite language and calling them with titles such as "Seor" (Mr.) or "Seora"

(Mrs./Ms.). "Por favor" (please) and "gracias" (thank you) are common phrases used to convey civility.

Personal Space: Be considerate of others' personal space, particularly in busy places. Maintain an acceptable distance during chats and avoid standing too near to people.

Punctuality: In Mexican society, being on time for appointments and social engagements is valued. However, it is normal for social gatherings to start later than expected, so some flexibility is advised.

Dress Code: Because Merida's environment is often warm, light and modest clothes is appropriate for most events. Consider wearing more modestly and covering shoulders and knees while visiting religious or formal locations.

Photography Etiquette: Always get permission before photographing individuals, particularly in intimate or personal settings. Some individuals may feel uneasy about having their images taken without their permission.

Respect for Sacred places: Be careful of the serious mood while visiting churches or religious places. Avoid having loud discussions and avoid from photographing religious rituals.

Tipping is customary in Merida. A 10-15% tip is recommended at restaurants. It is also traditional to tip tour guides, transportation, and hotel workers for exceptional service.

Bargaining is permitted in marketplaces and certain small businesses, but not in bigger stores or luxury venues. Approach negotiation with a nice demeanor and understand that it is not always anticipated.

Respect Local Traditions: Be mindful of local customs and traditions, particularly during festivals and festivities. Follow the established rites and show respect for cultural heritage if you participate.

Be Open and kind: Meridians are typically kind and open. A friendly demeanor and a cheerful attitude go a long way toward making genuine relationships with locals.

By adopting and respecting local traditions and etiquette, you will enrich your cultural experience in Merida, build goodwill with residents, and guarantee a smooth and comfortable travel around this dynamic city.

Basic Phrases and Expressions

Learning some basic phrases and expressions in the local language can greatly enhance your experience when visiting Merida. While Spanish is the primary language spoken in Mexico, the Yucatec Maya language is also prevalent in the region. Here are some useful phrases in both languages:

Spanish Phrases:

Hello - Hola

Good morning - Buenos días

Good afternoon - Buenas tardes

Good evening - Buenas noches

Please - Por favor

Thank you - Gracias

You're welcome - De nada

Yes - Sí

No - No

Excuse me - Disculpe

I'm sorry - Lo siento

How are you? - ¿Cómo estás? (informal) / ¿Cómo está? (formal)

I don't understand - No entiendo

Do you speak English? - ¿Hablas inglés? (informal) / ¿Habla usted inglés? (formal)

Where is...? - ¿Dónde está...?

How much does it cost? - ¿Cuánto cuesta?

Can you help me? - ¿Puedes ayudarme? (informal) / ¿Puede ayudarme? (formal)

Yucatec Maya Phrases:

Hello - Ba'ax ka wa'alik

Good morning - Ma'alob kin

Good afternoon - Ma'alob k'ajle'

Good evening - Ma'alob k'iin

Please - Ma'aloob

Thank you - Nusuba'

You're welcome - Ma'aloob kuxtal

Yes - Háan

No - Máan

Excuse me - Kóoben

I'm sorry - T'an úuch k'a'ana'

How are you? - ¿Bix yanikech? (informal) / ¿Bix yanik úuchben? (formal)

I don't understand - Ma' a sa'ala'an

Do you speak English? - ¿Ba'ax ka sajal óoxten? (informal) / ¿Ba'ax ka sajal u k'ab óoxten? (formal)

Where is...? - ¿Te'ele' in...?

How much does it cost? - ¿Juntúul ich k'iine'?

Can you help me? - ¿Ba'ax ka'alik in ts'o'onot? (informal) / ¿Ba'ax ka'alik k'ab in ts'o'onot? (formal)

Learning and using these phrases will show your appreciation for the local culture and make it easier to communicate with locals during your visit to Merida.

Currency and Banking Services

The Mexican Peso (MXN) is the country's official currency. When visiting Merida, it is important to be acquainted with the local currency and financial services. Here is some information to assist you with your financial requirements:

Currency exchange services are provided in Merida through banks, exchange offices (casas de cambio), and certain hotels. It is best to examine exchange rates and costs before proceeding with the transaction. Major currencies, such as US dollars and euros, are often accepted.

ATMs: ATMs are plentiful in Merida, and the majority accept foreign debit and credit cards. Look for ATMs that are part of major networks such as Visa, Mastercard, or Cirrus. Remember that certain ATMs may impose a fee for foreign withdrawals.

Credit Cards: Credit cards are frequently accepted at Merida's hotels, restaurants, stores, and other places. Visa and Mastercard are the most often accepted cards, but American Express may be accepted in limited quantities.

Banks: Major Mexican banks have branches in Merida. Monday through Friday, banking hours are normally from 9:00 a.m. to 4:00 p.m. Some banks may be open on Saturdays but with limited hours.

Traveler's checks: Although they are not as widely used as they once were, certain businesses may still take them. However, carrying a combination of cash and credit/debit cards is suggested for convenience.

Mexican Peso banknotes are available in denominations of 20, 50, 100, 200, 500, and 1,000 pesos. Coins are available in denominations of one, two, five, ten, and twenty pesos, as well as centavos (cents).

Security: Exercise caution while using ATMs and dealing with cash in public locations. Displaying large quantities of money or precious things should be avoided, and critical papers such as passports and travel documents should be kept safe.

Tipping is traditional in Mexico. In restaurants, it's customary to give a 10-15% tip, and paying cleaning workers is welcomed in hotels. Tipping tour guides and drivers for outstanding service is also traditional.

Remember to notify your bank of your trip intentions to Mexico in order to prevent any problems with using your cards abroad. Additionally, maintain emergency contact information for your bank and credit card firms on hand in case there are any issues with your accounts. Being prepared with local money and knowing the various banking services can make your financial experience in Merida more pleasurable.

CONCLUSION

Finally, the "Merida Travel Guide 2023 & Beyond" is a thorough and helpful resource that reveals the delights of this enthralling Mexican city. Merida entices visitors with its rich history and cultural legacy, from the grand architecture of Paseo de Montejo to the enigmatic Mayan ruins dispersed across the area.

The book has walked you through the ideal time to visit, vital travel recommendations, visa requirements, and practical information to ensure a smooth and pleasurable trip. You've visited a multitude of family-friendly sites, health retreats, and exhilarating outdoor excursions to meet the needs of every visitor.

Immerse yourself in local traditions and etiquettes, and enjoy the Meridians' warm hospitality as you dine on Yucatecan food and see traditional performances.

This book has equipped you with the information to make the most of your stay in Merida, whether you're exploring the splendor of Plaza Grande and the Cathedral of San Ildefonso or heading off the beaten road to hidden jewels.

Allow this book to be your trusty companion while you explore Merida's rich history, cultural riches, and natural marvels, enriching your experience and enabling you to truly enjoy the city's authenticity.

Set off on your Merida trip with a heart full of enthusiasm and a mind full of insights, and let the city's energy, warmth, and charm leave an unforgettable impact on your spirit.

Merida welcomes your arrival, eager to offer its incomparable beauty and create treasured moments that will live in your heart for years to come, from busy marketplaces to calm cenotes, ancient ruins to contemporary art. Good luck, and may your trip to Merida be nothing short of wonderful!